Transcendental Telemarketer

Poems

Beth Copeland

BlazeVOX [books]
Buffalo, NY

Transcendental Telemarketer by Beth Copeland

Copyright © 2012

Published by BlazeVOX [books]

Printed in the United States of America

Book design by Geoffrey Gatza

First Edition
ISBN: 978-1-60964-088-0
Library of Congress Control Number: 2011940044

BlazeVOX [books]
76 Inwood Place
Buffalo, NY 14209

Editor@blazevox.org

publisher of weird little books

BlazeVOX [books]

blazevox.org

2   4   6   8   0   9   7   5   3   1

BlazeVOX

for Phil

Acknowledgements

Acknowledgement is made to the following publications for poems that originally appeared in them:

Atlanta Review: "Misconception," "Negative Space"

Broken Bridge Review: "Pear Tree," "Transcendental Telemarketer"

Cairn: "Kimono," "Mikimoto Pearls"

The Christian Century: "Reflections in a Spoon"

Connotation Press: "After the Typhoon," "Buddhist Scroll," "The Great Wave Off Kanagawa," "Zin Zen"

Contemporary American Voices: "Drawing Lesson," "Nagasaki—July 4, 2006," "Polishing Silver"

e: The 2002 Emily Dickinson Awards Anthology: "Third Eye"

e: The 2003 Emily Dickinson Awards Anthology: "Orange"

Hunger Mountain: "The Bambi Canzone"

Iodine Poetry Journal: "What the Body Remembers"

Sunrise from Blue Thunder: A Pirene's Fountain Anthology: "The Great Wave Off Kanagawa"

Kakalak 2008: "Boolean Operators: Marriage"

The Kerf: "The Origins of Silk," "Purple Loosestrife"

The Ledge: "Self-Portrait as a House"

Main Street Rag: "Cerebus," "Maps"

Margie: A Journal of American Poetry: "My Life as a Slut"

North American Review: "Canzone"

Out of Line: "Kilim," "Orchid"

Peregrine: "Obi"

Pinesong Awards 2006: "Still Life With One Apple"

Pirene's Fountain: "Similitude," "Thumbnail Moon"

Prime Number: "Confession"

The Rambler: "And One More Thing …"

Vox: "Claire de Lunatic"

Table of Contents

Transcendental Telemarketer

I

"I decided to start anew, to strip away what I'd been taught."
—*Georgia O'Keeffe*

Still Life With One Apple

From earliest memory: one apple
in a bowl predating speech, spores

of sunlight floating on air like pollen
from the garden of Hesperides.

In childhood I wanted everything in pairs,
animals entering Noah's ark two by two,

the symmetry of hand in hand,
bride and groom.

I thought the apple needed another apple
or at least the company of an orange or pear,

that the apple was lonely, that everything—
even an apple in a bowl—

had a soul. Was it wrong to believe
the apple could suffer and bleed,

to project my own needs
onto that fruit?

To believe only a membrane
of matter and speed

separates blood from stone
and bone from apple seed?

To see the apple as a symbol
of the universal soul,

as in Georgia O'Keeffe's "Green
Apple on Black Plate,"

a study in simplicity?
Still Life With An Empty Bowl—

I ate the apple to make it whole.

Misconception

It was like catching a cold.
If he coughed without covering his mouth,
if he sneezed, you could have his baby,
or so I believed

at the age of nine when I read the chapter
on reproduction in a medical text. I knew the facts
of life had nothing to do with storks and bees,
but I couldn't figure out the mechanics

of sex, that tab A had to be inserted
into slot B like the cardboard figures cut
from the Rice Krispies box that always fell
apart when I tried to put them together.

Conception was a kind of weather
or photosynthesis: as leaves absorb sunlight
and turn green, I thought a man's floating spores
could penetrate a woman's pores,

that they could be on opposite sides of the room
just looking at each other or looking out the window.
One could be reading the newspaper and the other
playing *Heart and Soul* on the piano

when, *WHAM, BAM,* sperm and egg collide
and nine months later she becomes a mother.
I thought the microscopic sperm
could pass like germs from unwashed hands

contaminate a door knob, spoon or drinking glass,
or as Casper
floated through brick walls
on Saturday morning cartoons, believing

a wife could receive her husband's seed
like milkweed sown from the pod,
that every birth was a miracle, a gift from God,
that all you need is love.

Learning to Pray

I was told to close my eyes
and fold my hands like an unopened book.

I was not supposed to look
but sometimes I peeked

through downcast eyes
at steepled fingertips,

the double doors of thumbs
that opened and shut on all the people

in the sanctuary of palms.
After we read the one hundredth Psalm,

 the preacher said a prayer.
Amen.

I unfolded my hands,
and the church disappeared.

How many years did it take me to learn
what the restless child knew then?

Prayer isn't reverence in our hearts.
It's in our hands.

Confession

I stole another woman's only scarf—
        No, I didn't. I stole the line above to lead to the next
line, swiped like the challis scarf

lost in a church parking lot.
        It was black with a blue-and-white geometric print
like tiny Turkish tiles.

One Sunday I looked up from prayer
        and an old woman in the pew in front of me
was wearing my scarf!

Because it had been given to me
        by someone I loved, I couldn't let it pass,
so after church, I said, "You're wearing

my scarf," and she said, "Someone found it
        and said it looked like mine," adding insult to injury
since I didn't think my beautiful scarf

looked like it would belong to
        a woman wearing Hush Puppy shoes and a Brillo-pad
hairdo. "But it's not yours," I said.

"It's mine," so she took it off,
        handing it over as if she were giving me a gift
when the scarf had been mine to begin with.

I still wear it, especially
        on cold mornings when I need to wrap something warm
and familiar around my neck.

That happened many years ago
        when I still went to church and still believed
I was lost and needed God to find me.

My Life as a Slut

Age 6: A boy finds a penny on the playground. He says he'll give it to me if I go in a closet, take off all my clothes, and let him look. My sister says, "Don't," but I do it, anyway.

Age 21: My mother calls me a "harlot," "Jezebel," and "strumpet" after I stay out all night with my boyfriend. I roll my eyes and say, "If we're going to have this conversation, at least update your vocabulary. The word is 'slut.'"

Age 16: A teacher tells me to kneel in the girls' bathroom. Am I supposed to pray for forgiveness? I get sent home from school because my skirt doesn't touch the floor.

Age 27: I walk down the aisle in an off-white satin dress. It's snowing, and the next day I lose my voice.

Age 20: I have sex with three different men in one week. I write their names on my calendar in wisteria-blue ink.

Age 10: At recess I tell Tommy Faircloth I'm going to be a stripper when I grow up. Tommy tattles to the teacher, who scolds him and says I'm a good girl. I would never say a terrible thing like that.

Age 32: A man at my college reunion tells me a lot of other girls in our class were sluttier than I was. I feel like a failure.

Age 23: I fall in love with a Vietnam vet who plays guitar and writes bad poetry. I sleep with him on the first date. He dumps me for a frumpy girl who waits until the second date.

Age 9: I'm walking down the sidewalk wearing short-shorts, and a teenage boy leans out a car window and yells, "Call me when you're 16!"

Age 30: I buy a bar of *Saints and Sinners* soap in New Orleans. My husband says it's a rip-off.

Age 18: I get drunk at a party and lose my virginity. The next morning hot water runs down my thighs in a stream of silver and blood.

Age 5: I'm afraid of dogs, strangers, and the dark. Shadows cast by tree branches and leaves on the bedroom wall look like the devil's face. Do I hear footsteps in the stairwell? I'm afraid I'll die in my sleep. I know I'm going to Hell.

Belts

I

No, I won't
stand still
while she
whips me
with Daddy's
belt. She's mad
because I won't
clean my room
and said, "I hate
you, you ugly
old witch."
It's Saturday.
I want to watch
Mighty Mouse
and eat a frozen
Twinkie.
I run from room
to room as she
lashes at my legs,
leaping as if
we're playing
hop-scotch
without chalk
or rocks. When
he comes home,
I point at red
welts on
my legs. "See
what she did to
me." He
says, "You
deserved it."

II

He unbuckles
his belt, unzips
his jeans. I'm
drunk. I don't
want him to,
he's blonde with black
moles on his back
like dead flies.
It's Saturday
night, our first
date. I don't
move, I don't
say "No!"
or "Stop!"
He's on top
pushing
inside until
I break
in two: one
girl stays
on the bed
while the other
one floats
to the ceiling
to watch.
Whatever
you do,
you're
gonna get
what's
coming
to you.

Clair de Lunatic

19

When the moon is full
crazy things
happen: silver wolves

howl, owls hoot, people
fall in love
or knife each other,

women bleed in time
to ebb tides
and the linked rhythms

of sisters and friends,
men drink and
drive, children sleepwalk

into black mirrors,
waking up
on the other side.

Reflections in a Spoon

Hunger is a bowl of reflected light,
a concave mirror of flight,
an image reversed,
the breech birth
of an angel floating from Earth
feet first.

Accidental Angel

We meet by chance after more than twenty years
apart, pretending we don't remember that night in your bed,
lying heart to spine, entwined in seamless sleep as snow
pressed against the window, spiraling down like white
feathers from heaven, or that morning when we rose
from the blurred imprint of wings

on wrinkled sheets. Maybe I spread my wings
a little ... I was no angel in those years,
just another fallen woman who rose
in silence from your bed
and disappeared into the white
oblivion of burning snow.

Seeing you now, I remember the snow,
how it whirled on unfurled wings
of wind as we scraped a white
skin from the windshield. How many years
has it been? I remember making love in your bed,
a red lipstick rose

on the rim of a glass of rosé,
ostrich feathers of frost and snow
on your window when we left your bed
as strangers, as outspread wings
lifted us into the flurry of years
where memories fade to white ...

Leaving, I slipped and fell in the white
drifts, forming an accidental angel as I rose
like Chagall's bride into the blue horizon of years,
flying with violins, silver fish, a vase of lilacs and snow,
a woman floating without wings
above the bed.

We'll never speak of that night in your bed,
but our thoughts unroll like an empty white
scroll borne on the wings
of the angel that rose
from the snow
years

and years ago as we rose
from your bed, leaving white
wings in the snow.

Wisteria

How the word sounds like *mysterious*
and *wistful* combined,

how vines twine, counter-clockwise
around telephone poles

and twist around dying pines;
how flowers dangle

like amethyst pendants from pergola
posts, how branches

from a distance look like purple smoke
from unseen fires

on gnarled vines that tighten like wires
around a choking host.

Pear Tree

From my window I saw my neighbor's pear tree
covered in white blossoms. I thought it was snow.
When snow covered the pear tree's branches, I thought
I saw white petals unfold from buds of ice

covered in white blossoms. I thought it was snow.
When wind scattered snow from the pear tree's branches,
I saw white petals unfold from buds of ice.
Ivory petals drifted by my window.

When wind scattered snow from the pear tree's branches,
floating like glitter in a shaken snow dome,
ivory petals drifted by my window.
Star-white flowers shivered in a blurred season,

floating like glitter in a shaken snow dome.
The pear tree's blossoms, buds and branches froze as
star-white flowers shivered in a blurred season
of frost and inflorescence, blizzard and bloom.

The pear tree's blossoms, buds and branches froze. As
the seam between seasons curved into a lens
of frost and inflorescence, blizzard and bloom,
I thought I was seeing double, believing

the seam between seasons curved into a lens
clouded with breath. Was it spring? Was it winter?
I thought I was seeing double, believing
snow was falling as seafoam-white buds opened,

clouded with breath. It was spring. It was winter
when snow covered the pear tree's branches. I thought
snow was falling. As seafoam-white buds opened,
I saw my neighbor's pear tree from my window.

Purple Loosestrife

Loosestrife's taken over the wetlands, choking out
clover, bindweed, and chickory, its violet spreading
inviolate along marsh bank and roadside, burning
a streak through prairie and field. Wildfire's flower,
its purple blaze so invasive selling the plant is outlawed
in several Midwestern states, calls to mind
a friend who said, "Too much of a good thing

is dangerous," as if boundless joy could be restrained
and desire cordoned behind velvet ropes.
Loosestrife. Lose strife. Lythrum.
Life, reseeding itself in a surge of pure, unbridled
growth, its wild, unwieldy sprawl like the blood's
leap against the heart's muscled walls
in irrepressible hope.

Water Oak

Between earth and sky, a bare limb,
a sparrow hidden in the leaves.
No one knows what the wind feels

or what we feel when we fail, fall
bereft at being left to grieve. One leaf.
The stark outlines of trees limned

against blue stars. Limbic
selvages of sky, what's left
when the last leaf falls.

Conditional Constructs

If I am the dust on the windowpane,
you are the violet wave of light around the Japanese iris.

If you are the yellow pistil in the lily's white throat,
I am the highest note of the nightingale's Arabic song.

If I am the key to a door that doesn't lock,
you are the house in North Carolina next to railroad tracks.

If you are the scent of ripe peaches in a blue enamel bowl,
I am the sandalwood heart inside the peach.

If I am wisteria vines on a dead pine,
you are kudzu climbing the telephone pole.

You are the orbit of a falling stone.
I am the boat without oars in the middle of a silent lake.

Boolean Operators: Marriage

With names linked by AND the search ends:
Sun and moon, his and hers, wife and husband.

Wedding rings overlap in a Venn diagram.
Marriage is the shaded space within those bands.

The search expands with yours OR mine.
Mars or Venus, misaligned.

Refine the search to exclude all others.
Spouses, NOT lovers.

One cancels one.
A total eclipse of the sun.

Nikko Blue

I wrap the stems in waxed
paper, but the flowers wilt

in the car before I arrive, delft
globes drooping like deflated

balloons in the heat and humidity
of August afternoon.

You place them in a mason jar,
honoring my hope

that water is all hydrangeas
need to bloom

again. Later, we toss
flowers off the moon

deck, making a wish
as each miniature planet

Earth sails into the dark
woods, a lost world.

Russian Dolls

Self-contained: each memory nested in another
memory, moving backward into infinity
where nothing is too small or too far
removed to fit into the body
of linden or birch,
beginning with
today

as I struggle to remember who I was five minutes ago,
which babushka-wearing woman who shrinks
with each recursion is standing in
the doorway, which child
is hidden inside her
older clone,
which

version of the same story will be told this time, which
frame will hold the picture holding Droste's
portrait of a woman holding a tray
with her picture in a frame
around a tiny portrait
of the woman
like

Chinese boxes or an onion, the story within the story,
the body within the body, bone within bone,
eye within eye within eye within
the varnished shell of a doll
where a another doll
vanishes,
so

small the artist uses a magnifying glass to paint her eyelashes,
parted lips, her hand clutching a single rosebud,
her body opening to the child at the core
where it ends or begins (depending
on how you look at it) with
a glimpse of dark water
& blood.

II

"All of life is a foreign country." —Jack Kerouac

Obi

My sister brings me an antique obi from Kyoto.
Maybe this gift is her way of saying I should go back
to visit the country where we were born, to see gardens
of raked sand, Shinto shrines, and maples
with leaves shaped like a child's handprint.
I unwrap the sash of persimmon-colored silk
embroidered with gold chrysanthemums,
plum branches, and brocade fans like the paper
fan she folds and unfolds when she dances
the Odori with her hair pulled back
in a knot at the nape of her neck.

The nape of the neck is an erogenous zone
in Japan. Women wear the kimono loosely draped,
exposing the swan's slope of shoulder, the neck
whitened with rice powder. Once
a man kissed me there, saying, "It's so
warm, so soft." I never loved him. I guess
I'd been away from home too long to feel pleasure
or pain at the stork's bite, unlike the woman
who stepped from this pool of fallen silk
into the floating world of the past,
the gray sumi-e rain.

Kimono

Willow green waves billow on ivory sleeves
embroidered with pink paulownia leaves

threaded in silver, with a flame-colored phoenix,
its sickle feathers stitched

in gold. A woman wore this rinzu silk kimono
on her wedding day in Tokyo,

raising a ceremonial cup of sake to her lips,
head bowed as she sipped.

Now the kimono hangs on the wall above my bed,
its deep sleeves spread

like wings of the bride who became a white bird
and flew to the moon without a word.

Self-Portrait as a House

In kindergarten I drew a picture of a house—
one red square with two square windows like eyes
on either side of a brown door without a knob,
each window divided into four square panes,
topped by a triangular roof like a folded newspaper hat,
a black coil of smoke rising from the stovepipe chimney,
and my name printed at the bottom in block letters
anchoring my house to earth—BETH,
meaning *house* in Hebrew,

which may explain why I collect miniature houses
and line them up on shelves like Shinto shrines,
and why there are houses embroidered on guest towels
and a row of houses on the wallpaper border in my bathroom,
and why a house was the one thing I wanted when I grew up—
not a diamond ring, or car, or Imelda Marcos collection
of spike-heeled designer shoes—but a house,
a symbolic extension of the self,
a container for all the rooms of my life,

beginning with the prefabricated house in Fukuoka.
One night the roof blew off during a typhoon.
After that, we moved to a house where Japanese
children pressed their noses against the windows,
peering in at my sisters and me
when we had to take naps after lunch.
We hated going to sleep, so we'd jump
on our beds and pretend to be Sumo wrestlers
by wedging our underpants up our butt cracks.

I don't remember the house in Louisville
where we lived when I was three, but I recall the Campbell's Kids
on a soup label and eating Frosted Flakes and watching Howdy Doody
on TV and taking a bath with a Claribelle the Clown
washrag and the pink-eyed rabbit at the nursery school
where my best friend was a girl named Jeannie
and my boyfriend was a Chinese kid who accidentally
hit me in the head with a brick.
I had to have three stitches.

After we moved back to the house in Fukuoka,
I learned to print my name in English
and practiced writing
Japanese
characters
in
a
vertical
line.

When we moved to Wake Forest we lived
in a big white house with a wrap-around porch.
Once, some girls came over for a slumber party,
and everyone was scared when they heard my father
snoring downstairs, thinking it was Bluebeard's ghost.
I shone a flashlight on the ceiling,
slowly bringing a giant shadow hand down
to grab them. I wrote my name
on the wall inside my closet before we left

for Benares, where we lived in a bungalow
where geckos clung to the walls with tiny suction-cup feet,
and a rat we nicknamed Riki Tiki Tavi
squeezed through drainage holes to my sister's bedroom at night.
There were no screens on the windows to keep out mosquitos and flies,
no hot water, no refrigerator or oven, only a charcoal stove
where Abdul prepared our meals of water
buffalo and mashed potatoes molded
into swans with carrot slice beaks,

until we returned to the house in Wake Forest,
where my name was still written on the closet wall,
but the other eighth-grade girls thought I was weird
because I'd never heard of the Beatles and used the word "queer"
to refer to anything odd or unusual, and when the boy sitting behind me
said, "Eat me...eat me raw," I said, "Why would I want to do that?"
thinking he was talking about some "queer" form of cannibalism
practiced in redneck regions of the Appalachians,
which only encouraged him to keep pestering me

until we moved to the brick split-level house in Raleigh.
I had a basement room with a twin bed and small maple desk
where I wrote poetry late at night instead of studying
for chemistry tests, secretly wishing my name
was melodious like Amelia Rose or Meredith
or French like Solange or Yvette, instead of
Beth, a one-syllable name that can be uttered
in a single breath. Beth, as stolid and plain
as the four-square house with forest green shutters

where I lived when my children were young,
after a decade of dorm rooms and apartments before I was married.
Once, a drunk man at a bar said, "Baby, you're built like a brick
shit house," a backhanded compliment, I guess,
since to be a house, even an outhouse,
is to be grounded, rooted to earth,
and I was ready to settle down and stay in one place
instead of traveling with only the contents of a suitcase
and a map I never figured out how to read,

even when I held it sideways to read the names
of North-South streets that, like Japanese, are written vertically
instead of left to right or West to East.
The house in Chicago was on a one-way street
which made it hard to give directions to anyone
who visited, but it had an old oak staircase I stripped
to a Norwegian blonde sheen and an enclosed porch painted white,
with wicker chairs and plantation blinds that reminded me
of the house in Wake Forest that I love best

of all the houses I've lived in and left.
Now I live in a blue house without geckos, rats or ghosts,
in a sleepy suburb where neighbors drive into attached garages
and are never seen. This may be the last house I'll inhabit on Earth,
except for the house of flesh and bone I was given at birth,
along with my name, Beth.

A name that can be uttered in a single breath.
In this house with charcoal-gray shutters.
In this house that rhymes with death.

Orchid

Flight attendants on Royal Thai Airlines
handed us orchids as we boarded the plane,
tropical purple blooms with spurred labellum
like the sanctum of a woman's private parts.
I was thirteen when I pinned that flower on
my heart, imagining my hand was Ricky
Nelson's, that someday he would sing "Travelin'
Man" and sweep me away in a bouffant skirt
of crinolines and wisteria chiffon.
We would slow dance at my high school prom, and then...

What did I know? A child suspended between
two worlds, breathing Himalayan oxygen
in the pressurized cabin, while in Bangkok's
brothels a girl my age was raped, the membrane
of childhood brutally torn; then, that petal
of flesh was sutured, surgically restored
so she could be deflowered again—sealed, sold
as a born-again virgin when the wound healed.
As I pinned the orchid to my blouse, a drop
of blood fell from its stem to the white napkin.

Maps

"To be lost is only a failure of memory." —Margaret Atwood

I love the antique maps no one follows
now that the world isn't flat,

the twin spheres of the old world
and the new, quilled on vellum,

the yellowed routes to China and the Indies
matted and framed on library walls.

Even the practical Rand-McNally
road maps, so hard to refold

once unfolded, direct us to Alpha,
Summit and Good Hope

on highways plotted
like a child's puzzle of connecting dots.

I love to read bas-relief maps
of mountains with my fingertips

like the blind read Braille,
to chart heat and rainfall

with solar maps of green,
ocher and taupe.

****

As a child I ran a finger
along the spinning globe, telling myself

where it stops, that's where I'll go,
touching the grosgrain ribbon

of the equator in that Ouija world,
ending up on the Ivory coast,

Barbados, or a rainforest
in Brazil or Borneo.

In school I traced the veins
of my wrist with a fountain pen

as the teacher pulled down a chart
and pointed to the Nile,

Egypt, the land of papyrus,
pyramids, and crocodiles,

following blue rivers of blood
flowing back to the heart.

※※※※※※

We follow color-coded blocks
in the shopping mall, modern

hieroglyphs depicting shops, restrooms,
and food stalls, landmarks—

The Gap, Victoria's Secret, and Sears—
symbols and legends

guiding those who are lost
back to the start

with an arrow and the message:
You Are Here.

Buddhist Scroll

Calligraphy
flows
down
an old scroll
I bought at
Tenjin-san
like willow
branches
bending
to water.
No one
knows what
it means.
The merchant
says it's poetry
written in
a woman's
hand —black
brush strokes
on paper
the color
of ashes.

Shibui,
as the Japanese
say, that
untranslatable
quality of
restraint.
It doesn't
matter
that no
one can
translate
"grass
writing,"
that the
cursive
is too faint
and feathery
to read
because
language
is more
than

meaning:
it's the image
of a woman's
hand
moving
down
the page
as if
words
could
mean
something
without
meaning
something
more
than rain
on a gray
window
pane.

Mikimoto Pearls

"We are one planet, a single organism. What happens on this floor makes a difference everywhere. For the entire universe with its countless galaxies is the setting for this pearl of pain." —Madeleine L'Engle

Mikimoto pearls—
a strand of silent prayers
on a single breath.

The history of the pearl
is a life of suffering.

******

Minimalist style:
A room with white walls, one black
circle on a scroll.

Time is an infinite line
of abacus-bead moments.

******

White nights of worry.
Craters of ice on the moon.
A cup of warm milk.

Obsession's a rosary
of fear and anxiety.

******

Daredevil spider
plunges on a bungee cord
of sunlight and dust.

What holds us up? What keeps us
from falling, what safety belt?

******

Your name written on
a grain of rice. A map of
the world on a leaf.

The future condensed into
DNA's double helix.

******

White-tipped gray feather.
Where did it come from, what wing
dipped in heaven's ink?

I mail this letter to you
without a return address.

******

Kusahibiri,
the Japanese grass lark sings
in the key of G.

To hear the Earth's vibrations
converge in a single note.

******

Rice-planting season.
Albumin-white, the full moon
rises in the east.

Dreams are the silkworm's cocoon,
the spider's spirit ladder.

******

From a dragon's egg.
From an elephant's stomach.
From a heron's beak.

Where does creation begin?
In a holy equation.

******

In a drop of rain.
In Fibonacci's golden
string —1 0 1

1 0 1 0 1
1 0 1 1 0 ...

******

In the worm's furrow.
In the vortex of the wind.
The voice of God.

No one knows how this story
began or how it will end.

******

The dragonfly's wing
is a sheer kimono sleeve
woven from water.

*"All things are impermanent.
They arise and pass away."*

******

What begins as a
blister in the universe
becomes a planet.

Microcosm of the world—
precious, Bodhisattva pearl.

Nagasaki—July 4, 2006

Rain falls on the Atomic Bomb Museum
where radiation-scarred angels
from Urakami Cathedral
weep behind glass
with statues of headless saints,
stained glass shards,
a melted rosary,
a charred rice bowl,
a child's scorched robe,
a steel helmet with the remains of a skull,
a clock stopped by the blast.

Rain falls on the shoreline
where a girl once drew circles in the sand,
trying to remember her mother's face,
on the earth where the dying cried for water,
on a watchman's shadow burned into a wall,
a twisted ladder leading to the sky,
on the Vault for the Unclaimed Remains of Victims,
a camellia tree that survived the flames,
on the black cenotaph at ground zero,
umbrellas blown inside-out
with wind.

Rain falls on camphor trees at the Sanno Shrine,
on stones inscribed with names of the dead,
a chain of a thousand origami cranes,
the statue of a mother and child,
the Fountain of Peace where water flows
in the wing-beats of a dove,
on the city where 70,000 people died.
While school children pose for photographs,
holding fingers up in a V of peace,
North Korea fires seven long-range missiles
into the Japan Sea.

The Great Wave Off Kanagawa

We guess what happens
next: the wave breaks
on fishing boats and men
rowing against its wake.

Hokusai caught the arc
of the wave as a freeze
frame for Fuji's snow
capped peaks, a foil

for white crests
crashing into fractals
of foam on fishermen
like ashes from blue

flames in that split
second while we wait
with breath held, still
praying they'll reach

Edo Bay with silver
sardines and live
mackerel at the market
near the wooden bridge.

After the Typhoon

Everywhere, dead branches, fallen trees,
the smell of red dirt, earthworms, wounded
wood. If we could reverse the wind, we would
uncoil the waters of the world, let it whirl
like a spinning top set loose on the sidewalk
after rain has washed away chalked outlines
of words, bodies, or hop-scotch squares: SKY
BLUE is where we want to live instead of
in this gray, wool-wound ball of worsted
worry that's worse than the worst
whirlwind we'll ever survive.

Canzone

Agha Shahid Ali, I'm reading "Lenox Hill," the canzone
you wrote before you died, as your mother was dying, dreaming
of dying elephants in sedated sleep. No one writes canzones
now that you are gone. "Canzone?"
they ask. "What's that? Some kind of pizza?" No,
that's *calzone.* The canzone
is an Italian lyric with repeated end words. Mine are *canzone,*
dreaming, no, mother, and *Kashmir.* Yours are *elephants, mother,*
Kashmir, universe, and *die. Mother*
is universal, a word that may be used in my canzone
without apology, but *Kashmir*
belongs to you. *Kashmir*

is such a beautiful word that I must steal it. *Kashmir.*
The word is a sapphire in the maharaja crown of your canzone.
I've never seen the Krishna-blue mountains of Kashmir,
but when I whisper the word, I believe I am there. *Kashmir.*
Once, I was as close as Varanasi, dreaming
of a houseboat floating on Lake Dal in Kashmir.
Our friends in Varanasi said we should go to Kashmir
to escape the heat of the plains, but we never went. No,
we never saw the Gardens of Shalimar. I don't know
why we never traveled to the saffron fields of Kashmir.
That was long ago, but I remember my mother
spoke of spending a holiday in Srinigar. My mother

shopped in Viswanath bazaar for my grandmother's
ivory pashmina shawl of cloud-soft cashmere
woven with threads of warm breath binding mother
to child (in life, in death) and child to mother.
You write with longing of that bond in your canzone:
"Are you somewhere alive, somewhere alive. Mother?"
Before dying of the cancer that later took your life, your mother
dreamed a *"blizzard-fall of ghost-elephants."* Is dreaming
a rehearsal for death's descent? Did dreaming
of Mihiragula's elephants prepare your mother
for her fall from Pir Panjal's cliffs? Did she know
that you would soon follow her into that abyss? No,

I don't think she knew. I hope she didn't know.
The elephant-gray tumor in your mother's
brain soon burgeoned from grief within yours. No,
she surely would have wept if she had known. *"No!"*
You buried your mother's body in the Vale of Kashmir.
Where did they bury you? I need to know.
We never met, but I feel as if I know
you after reading your canzone.
Your elegant, elegiac canzone.
What will we do now that you are gone? No
one writes canzones. No one is dreaming
of a dying woman dreaming

of dying elephants. No one is dreaming
of blue mountains in the morphine sleep of dying. No
one is dreaming your mother's dreams, but the dreaming
god of the Upanishads is dreaming
the universal dream of life. Your mother's
death is a dream Vishnu is dreaming,
and we are the dreamers in that dream, dreaming
on a bridge of breath across the Jhelum River in Kashmir.
In death and in dreams she returned to Kashmir.
Kashmir is dying, but the world is dreaming,
blind to its destruction. Shahid, my canzone
can not compare to your canzone

chanted as kaddish for the dead, your canzone
sung as a muezzin's call from the minarets of Kashmir:
"The Beloved leaves one behind to die." No
stanza can express the exile's longing for the mother-
land as does your passage into death, your Sufic dreaming.

Kilim

An unknown woman wove this rug in Samarkand,
a map of the stars written in the palm of her hand.

A woman's life intertwined with the running vine,
the leaf-and-rosette garland.

Daily she sat on scaffolding boards at the loom.
Her agile hands worked in time to Allah's command.

Her breath lingers in the warp and weft of the wool.
Her fingers flew like birds above a nest, strand over strand.

Her fingerprints vanished in vats of blood, saffron, and wild pistachio,
becoming the sunburst, the palm tree, the dervish cloud band.

The vase with pomegranate branches is a symbol of fertility.
Did she have children? Did she love her husband?

Here is a field within a field, a border of vermilion dragons.
A stylized hourglass woven without falling grains of sand.

These zigzag designs are the seven steps to Paradise,
the Z that symbolizes life, delivered from Fatima's hand.

The Origins of Silk

A child's voice whispers in twisted threads
of this sandwashed silk blouse, in sleeves slipped on
and off. It's the sound of steam, monsoon rain,
or a child's tears falling as she ladles
cocoons from vats in Ramanagaram,
dipping her hands in boiling water
to remove the skeins. It's the sound of silk

tearing, skins shed, death. The truth's not always
beautiful. No matter how much I wish
these moth-winged sleeves could lift effortlessly
from sweat shop looms, it wouldn't be the truth.
This fine, gossamer cloth is woven from
an orphan's wounds, from the dying silkworm
at the center of this unwinding thread.

****

Which came first, the white moth or golden egg?
The larva uncurls from its global shell,
feeding on mulberry leaves until it
molts, inching from its old, condom-sloughed skin.
Metamorphosis is the silkworm's form
of reincarnation—ova, larva,
pupa, imago—avatars of one

Vedic god, spinning on a cosmic thread.
The pupa sleeps in Egyptian linen,
waiting for resurrection from the dead.
Finally, the soul rises from its shrouds —
the moth breaks free of its cloud-spun cocoon,
unfurling ghostly wings. *Bombyx mori,*
a child's voice whispers in twisted threads.

Mori, a state of dormancy or death.
The silk moth's flightless life passes without
sleep or the jade-green nourishment of leaves.
Its only purpose is to propagate
the species, to flutter pale wings, and mate.
Death is a potent aphrodisiac,
arousing consummation on the wings

of war or genocide. Survivors of
the Holocaust speak of lovers coupling
beneath a canopy of ashes in
the camps, clinging to flesh as fragile as
a web of dust or the last frozen breath
of a woman who might have touched the seam
of this sandwashed silk blouse, its sleeves slipped on

****

and off in Dachau's poison showers.
History demands that we remember
all this—the names of those who vanished from
Cambodia's killing fields and the streets
of Sarajevo, the human shadow
burned into Hiroshima's stone stairway,
the napalmed villages of Vietnam—

an endless reel of human suffering.
We can watch the 24-hour news
on CNN, until we fall asleep
in front of the screen as burning Towers
collapse on prerecorded footage of
9-11, before waking to turn
it off. It's the sound of steam, monsoon rain,

******

a world still breathing. Our grief is nothing
new to the people of Afghanistan,
who've suffered such losses long before this
strike at America's security.
Now, our lives are sewn to theirs with sutures
of surgical silk—widow to widow,
orphan to orphan—tied with threads of blood

and mourning to women in blue burqas,
children without hands and feet, with stumps wrapped
in white gauze, mujahedeen with Russian
Kalashnikovs. What is the difference
between our suffering and theirs, between
the tears of a firefighter's daughter
and a child's tears falling as she ladles

******

water in Pakistan's refugee camp?
There are no borders on grief's continent,
no tribal bonds or nationalities
beyond the ligatures of tragedy.
The olive-eyed girl on the cover of
National Geographic informs us
that those beneath the veil are human, too,

and we are connected by living threads
to them, and to children sold into silk's
bondage in Karnataka's black market,
working 12-hour days for $3
a week in steaming, dirty factories.
Twelve-year-old Naushad, who was boiling
cocoons from vats in Ramanagaram,

****

asked for a day off. He was set on fire
with kerosene and burned over eighty
percent of his body. That's only one
atrocity in the warped fabric of
a cruel industry. Thousands of young
children work, eat, and sleep on factory
floors littered with the rotting flesh of worms.

Some believe only a child's hands can feel
when strands have loosened enough from the silk
cocoons to be unwound, twisted and reeled.
The children stand on stools so they can reach
the stoves, stirring bubbling pots of cocoons.
The reelers are not allowed to use spoons.
Dipping her hands in boiling water,

Savita lifts hot cocoons from the vat.
Her hand is a blistered brocade of scars.
Is it her whisper you hear in the silk
blouse you're wearing, or is it Ganga's sigh
as she sits on a concrete slab from dawn
to dark, spinning endless thread on spindles
held between her toes? It's the vibrato

of Varanasi silk—Sunshine and Shade,
Ripples of Silver, Moon and Stars, Peacock's
Neck, Nightingale's Eyes—intricate brocades
woven by children Misra describes as
"cage-birds...condemned from their very birth to
be captive workers," youth hired as hands
to remove the skeins. It's the sound of silk.

****

Empress Hsi Ling-Shi discovered silk when
a cocoon fell into her cup of tea
as she sat beneath mulberry trees of
the Imperial Gardens. The cocoon
unraveled into a single thread when
she pulled it from her cup. Enchanted by
its luster, she gathered silk from thousands

of cocoons to weave the Emperor's robe,
or so the story goes. Silk's origins
are probably less romantic than this
legend embroidered with Mandarin
crests and dragons. The authentic version
is unknown, composed of many loose threads
tearing, skins shed, death. The truth's not always

****

written in elegant calligraphy
on silkscreen scrolls. There are many versions
of this story and all of them are true.
Some say the Yellow Emperor Huang-Ti
discovered silk; others give the Empress
credit. Some tales elevate Hsi Ling-Shi
to heaven, where she reigns as the goddess

of silk. For thousands of years the Chinese
nobility kept the secret of silk
production until an Imperial
princess smuggled silkworm eggs in her crown
when she married the sultan of Khotan.
Spun from one common thread, these legends are
beautiful. No matter how much I wish

****

this sandwashed silk blouse was woven from clouds,
from water running over river rocks,
or from the lint rinsed off mulberry leaves,
as Pliny believed, silk originates
in an insect's salivary gland, spun
from the silkworm's secretions as it sleeps
within its cocoon, woven with a child's

wounded hands. In Kanchipuram children
labor in airless rooms, inhaling dust
and sulphur fumes from vats of turmeric,
safflower and indigo, dreaming of
life beyond the selvages of bondage
to the flying shuttle and reed, wishing
these moth-winged sleeves could lift effortlessly

****

from their hands onto the arms of women
shopping at Lord & Taylor, women who
don't think about the origins of silk.
They don't see Ganga spinning thread, waiting
for a full moon when she will finally
get a day off. They don't see Savita's
blistered hands or Naushad's burning body

as they try on blouses, turning to check
their reflections in dressing room mirrors.
We see what we want to see, believing
that beauty is created from beauty,
and if someone said children sewed this blouse,
or this "Italian Silk" was imported
from sweat shop looms, it wouldn't be the truth.

******

The universe of the Vedas is one
continuous length of fabric woven
by two sisters, Day and Night, creating
a grid of light and shadow on their loom:
"They sit beside the warp and cry, 'weave forth,
weave back.'" There's an underside for every
pattern, a reversal, or reaction

to every action on this karmic plane.
As Savita rises from her pallet
on the factory floor, a woman on
the other side of the world is sleeping
beneath feathers and a white silk duvet.
Savita removes the boiling skeins
this fine gossamer cloth is woven from.

******

The raga of silk is the rhythm of
shuttle and reed—Shantung, charmeuse, chiffon.
Dupioni reeled from double cocoons.
Pongee, organza, georgette, grenadine.
Damask with muted tone-on-tone roses.
Scroll-patterned brocade from Ajanta caves.
Crinkled rice-paper lissé. Mousseline

de soie, watered moiré, and crepe de Chine.
Tissue silk with silver borders woven
from the tears of children who will never
go to school or play in the afternoon,
as other children do. Slowly, the moth's
unformed wings unfold in cloth woven from
an orphan's wounds, from the dying silkworm.

****

We wrap ourselves in winding sheets of silk,
oblivious to the misery of
children on the other side of the world—
Ganga, Savita, Naushad. What does their
suffering have to do with us? Why should
we care about what happens to people
in India, Afghanistan, Iraq?

Because what happens to them is linked to
our survival by overlapping threads.
At every crossing of one thread over
another we are choosing life or death
for ourselves and our sisters and brothers
on a tapestry of peace or bloodshed
at the center of this unwinding thread.

Cerebus

"Cry havoc and let slip the dogs of war."
—Shakespeare

What do the howling hounds hear that we can't?
The moon sharpens its sword on the Earth's stone.
Palm trees on the shores of the Tigris stand sentinel,
silently releasing sweet dioxide into nightscope green air.
In the mountains Kurdish children shiver beneath battered tents
of plastic sheeting, ravens spread petrol black wings.
We cross desert sands to burning oil wells,
poised on banks of poison water that corrodes everything
but hooves of apocalyptic horses, wheels of humvees and tanks.
When we reach the adamantine gates of Iraq
it's too late to turn back.

For the Poets of Afghanistan

Your words are beautiful, O poets of Kabul and Kandahar.
Rumi's answering word is a pointed sword.

Your children duel with rhyme in the yellow dust.
Their poems explode like poppies from the barrels of guns.

Rabeha Balki wrote her last poem in her own blood,
dying for forbidden love: "Eat poison,

but taste sugar sweet." Nadia Anjuman's poems
survived the Taliban, but she was murdered

for the crime of being a woman and writing
ghazals: "My wings are closed and I cannot fly.

I am an Afghan woman and must wail."
Listen. A snowfinch sings in the ruins of Herat.

White doves at the Blue Mosque in Mazar-e-Sharif
fly from stones: the dead have the last word.

III

All water has a perfect memory and is forever trying to get back to where it was.”—Toni Morrison

Negative Space

It's where I go when I zone
out, entranced, the entrance to ozone

blue, that Orphic note, the Om
of snow on snow, zinc-white

Zen hole in the inkless
oval of the O or zero.

It's the helium halo around
the moon, the echoing O, O, O,

Rimbaud's omega
of the hallowed vowel,

the ohm of the dial tone,
the Zenith screen

dissolving into fields of white
noise and burning snow.

It's the osmosis of light
on Sugimoto's photographs of fog

taken morning, afternoon and night
over the Ligurian sea,

opaque layers of vapor and mist
exposed on cibachrome.

It's the gesso-white canvas
no brush stroke disturbs,

the vanishing point where heaven
and earth converge

in the void of the universe,
in the holy word.

Drawing Lesson

for my son, Joe, at age 16

Outside your window the sky looks like you rubbed the edge
of charcoal across it, smudged with sfumato clouds.
You sketch from a photograph taken
on Christmas morning when you were two
and your sister was five. A contour of smoke
curls around your cherub cheek.
You've captured your sister's smile with a soft curve,
but the crown of her head floats off the page
as if its flat surface could never hold the memory
of that moment within such limited space.

Do you think it's a mistake to spill over the edge
where the image bleeds into negative space?
When your mind goes as blank as untouched parchment,
when you follow your hand wherever it leads—to the empty space
beyond the margins of safety—when you risk falling
from the horizon line of the world
into the ellipse of the earth's revolution,
when the skylark bones of your hand soar in an arc
of swift, penciled flight, when you trace the line
of rain falling straight from heaven to earth,
you will know how to draw from life.

Third Eye

Like Tara, Tibetan mother of all buddhas, born
from Avalokiteshvara's teardrop, with a third eye

in the middle of her forehead like a Hindu *tilak*
or skull painted in a cyclops eye above

Frida Kahlo's witchy black eyebrows,
with stigmata-like peepholes in her palms and soles,

all mothers are blessed with x-ray vision,
spotting vodka bottles, zip-lock bags of cannabis,

cigarettes, and *Playboy* magazines under beds,
red Fs rounded into counterfeit Bs on algebra tests.

Mothers place peacock-eyed palms on children's foreheads,
reading thoughts and nonexistent fevers like The Amazing Kreskin.

"You're not sick," they scold, waving airport-scanning-wand
hands over cool, unbeaded brows. "Get out of bed.

You didn't finish your homework, did you?
That's the real reason you don't want to go to school."

Like the Zen monk who stared at a white wall
for so long he finally cut off his own eyelids

to stay awake, mothers wait in dark living rooms
with toothpick-propped eyelids peeled for teenaged kids

sneaking in past curfew, with hawk eyes that stalk
skulking culprits like eerie eyes in museum portraits

that are always watching you no matter what
covert corner of the room you move to;

with removable eyes like the eye of Ra, the Egyptian sun-god
who sent his eye (which he could pop out like a contact lens)

to search the night sky for his lost children.
By the time the eye returned, Ra had grown another eyeball

in its socket, so he stuck the wandering eye in the center
of his forehead where it rules the universe as the Sun.

So, if you still think you're flying under the radar screen,
evading the mother of all video surveillance cameras,

think again. Reach into your pocket and take out a one dollar bill.
An unblinking green eye floats at the top of the pyramid—

Ra's eye, or Tara's, watching over all
of us, the budding buddhas, the lost kids.

Evil Eye

I never gave you the paperweight
with a silver *hamsa*, Miriam's hand
or Fatima's (depending on your faith).

The first time you drew a cross
in the palm of my hand,
saying a prayer

to protect me from
burning, we were drinking
black chianti at Finelli's,

and I felt a flame of blood
fly from your heart
to my hand.

I had to glance down
at the white tablecloth to break
our gaze Later, you said

people in Greece and Italy
still wear charms—silver horns,
red cords with glass beads,

Osiris's eye—to protect
themselves from blue-green
eyes like mine. I'm sorry

I didn't buy this paperweight
until it was too late.

Transcendental Telemarketer

Congratulations! You have won an all expense paid vacation to
Paradise, Heaven, Nirvana, Valhalla, Olympus or the Promised Land.
To claim your prize you must pay a one-time activation fee of $99.95.
Provide your VISA, Discover, or MasterCard account number at the tone ... *No,
thank you* ... and you will receive a complimentary offer of enlightenment
salvation, and deliverance from...*Sorry, I don't think so...* Ring... *Hello.*

Congratulations! You have won... *I'm not interested. Goodbye...* Ring... *Hello.*
Ms. Copeland, please do not delay. This offer of eternal life is limited to
pre-approved customers on a first-come, first-served basis. Enlightenment,
salvation and an all expense paid trip to Heaven, Paradise or the Promised Land
can be yours only if you act today. May I process your prize? ...*No.*
Have you ever dreamed of a transcendental getaway? Call 1-800-555-5555,

and you'll receive our bonus of a Good News Bible, Torah, Koran, and the Five
Classics of Confucius, including the I-Ching or Book of Changes... Hello?
Earth to Ms. Copeland... Isn't this unbeatable value too good to refuse? ...*No.*
If you sign up today you'll receive the mystical secrets of the Cabala, too.
This offer is available to residents of California, New York and Maryland
only and includes first-class, luxurious accommodations, enlightenment,

and all gratuities. *Sorry, I'm not interested ...* Buddha attained enlightenment
while sitting under a bodhi tree, and Mohammed's followers observe the Five
Pillars of Faith so they can earn rewards in the hereafter. Well, Ms. Copeland,
what are you waiting for? A one-way ticket to the Inferno or Hell? ... *Oh,
God! Stop calling me! I told you I'm not interested, but you continue to
call and disturb me...* Ms. Copeland, you should know

this offer comes with a lifetime guarantee and cannot be undersold...*No!
I said no. I don't want to go...* May I ask why you'd forego enlightenment,
rapture and breathtaking views? A blissful, once-in-a-lifetime cruise to
Heaven, Nirvana or Paradise can be yours for an activation fee of only $99.95.
We'll take care of all the details; the rest is up to you... *No! ...* Ring... *Hello.*
Congratulations! You have won an all expense paid vacation to the Pure Land

of Amida Buddha, Heaven, Nirvana, Paradise or the Promised Land.
How many times do I have to tell you? No! When I say no I mean no!
Ms. Copeland, as an incentive just for you, we'll include a golden halo
and white wings, but only if you act today and accept this offer of enlightenment,
salvation and deliverance from evil, and pay the activation fee of $99.95.
Please provide your VISA, Discover or MasterCard ... *What do I have to*

do to get you to stop calling me? I said no! (Exasperated, Beth Copeland
counts to ten.) *1, 2, 3, 4, 5...* Ring... *Hell, no. I'm not answering the damn phone!*
6, 7, 8, 9... At the tone you'll receive enlightenment.

Postcards From Paradise

"Paradise is exactly where you are right now ... only much, much better."
Laurie Anderson

We slept for hours, waking whenever we felt like it,
baking bread in the morning, kneading dough into loaves,

sharing the ritual of coffee and the newspaper,
drinking wine the color of sunlight

as we soaked in the hot tub under a dome of stars.

We tried to identify lizards and birds—the green anole
with its watermelon-colored dewlap puffing in and out,

the indigo bunting hovering at the feeder with turquoise wings
that are really black, but in paradise we see what we want to see

through the feathers of belief
where black is blue, the color of bliss, not grief.

Orange

Unrhymed, orange stands alone like a man without
the chime of a woman's voice in his house.

It's the color of sunlight and blood seen through closed eyelids,
of marigolds, Mexican sunflowers, and Monarch butterflies,

of Dreamsicle clouds drifting across the skyline at dusk,
of tangerines, tiger lilies, trumpet vines, and rust.

It's the glowing globe that opens
in his hand, lobe by lobe,

identical, but not quite, like the slant rhyme
of southern light on tamarind and pine.

It's the citrus scent of gin and Seville bitters
as he peels the rind, as each segment splits on its seam

without tearing, as he pares the white Valencian lace
of the inner skin from a crescent of fire

and tastes the summer heat, the heart's desire.
If only you were there to share its sweetness ...

He would give you the moon and the stars if you asked.
He divides the sun. He offers you half.

Lines That End in Sorrow

After years of sleeping with a knife under my pillow,
I fell in love. We drank White Russians and slow
danced to "Will You Still Love Me Tomorrow?"

I could have been Clara with a mouth like Cupid's bow
or Claribel Alegria who compared the poet to a pitiless crow.
He tied snow peas to bamboo stakes in a straight row

but rabbits ate the leaves and the pods didn't grow.
I wrote four words on torn envelopes*: Sorrow.
Woe. Wisteria. Willow.*

Flash forward—Now
we walk by cotton fields where the window
of time is still open. He picks a blossom of snow

and hands it to me as an offering. If you ask me how
this poem ends, I'll tell you the truth: I don't know.

The Bambi Canzone

Your ex-girlfriend, "Bambi,"
is beautiful and has double D-cup boobs.
Of course, her name isn't really Bambi,
but I like to call her Bambi
because she looks like one in the photo
I found in the bedside drawer. Bambi
sounds so bubbleheaded and bimboesque. Bambi
poses in snug, butt-hugging shorts with her tank top
pulled over her head. No bra! She liked being on top,
you said, boobs bouncing as she straddled you. Bambi
had multiple orgasms. I don't want to think
about her in bed with you, but I do. I think

about her too much. I feel bad when I think
about how much you loved buxom, bootielicious Bambi.
You say it's my problem, that I obsess too much and think
about her more than you do. You say you don't even think
about her that much anymore, that big boobs
aren't that important, and you think
my B-cup breasts are beautiful, too. If you think
I'm such a bona fide babe, why isn't my photo
next to your bed? Why is her picture
there, instead? Am I second best? I think
of how you ask me to slowly lift my top
over my head when I undress, just as she pulls her top

up in that snapshot, and I wonder if the top-
over-the-head move gets you so hot because it makes you think
of her, and if you still long for her when I'm on top
because she had multiple orgasms when she was on top,
but I do not. Will you ever love me as much as you loved Bambi?
Big bosomed, bombshell-bodied Bambi. How can I ever top
someone as bodaciously sexy as your ex? When I pull my top
over my head, do you compare my B-cup boobs
to her big bazongas? Her boobs
are huge, spilling over her bikini top
in another photo
taken at the beach. You kept that Kodak

moment, too, and a glamour shot
of bleached blond Bambi in a baby blue crop top.
Those photos
bother me, but not as much as that Polaroid
of her boobs. After she broke up with you, you couldn't think
of anything but Bambi. Did you gaze at her picture
with lust and longing? I wish I'd never seen those photographs.
I wish I'd never seen busty, Bunny-
wannabe Bambi
posing braless in the snapshot,
brazenly exposing her Barbie-doll boobs.
It's not just her boobs

I envy, even though her boobs
are beautiful. When I found that Polaroid
I saw her flat little belly, too. She has big boobs
but wears a size 2. I wish I'd never seen her boobs.
It's bad enough seeing her cleavage in a bikini top,
but a snapshot of her boobs ...
Why'd you keep that picture of her boobs?
You say I'm the woman you love, but I don't think
you really do. Do you still love her? I think
you do. You kept that snapshot of her boobs.
You kept a pair of Bambi's
black lace panties, too. The Queen B

left them on the floor. You say you forgot Bambi's
stuff was still in your drawer, but I think
you kept her panties and X-rated photo
because you loved her more with her top
pulled up, with her double D-cup boobs.

Bob's Side of the Story

I never saw it coming. One day she was the one
I would marry and be with forever and then *BAM*—she was gone.

Yes, she was beautiful—you've seen her picture so you know—
but that wasn't why I couldn't let go.

It's because I never understood why she dumped me,
how she could love me one day, and the next day—*See*

you in the funny papers, Bob. Or how we could go to bed
together and she said she loved me and then after a Dead

concert she said, *What am I going to do about you?*
as if I were a blue-winged fly to shoo

away or swat. I guess I held on so long
because I didn't understand how she could come on so strong

and then make a U-turn without any warning,
how we could be lovers one night and the next morning—

Adios, amigo—it was over.
Yes, it's true. I loved her,

but I don't anymore. Maybe I shouldn't have kept
her topless picture and black lace panties after I slept

with you, but it wasn't because I loved her more.
It was because she opened and shut the door

on me so quickly it seemed
as if everything happened in a Fellini movie or dream.

I had to pinch myself—did it happen or didn't it?
Didn't she say she loved me? Didn't she say I fit

inside her like a finger in a glove?
What was that all about if it wasn't love?

Haiku

Vodka air, glass sky.
Trees split with cleavers of ice.
Winter's clarity.

Zin Zen

Red flannel pajamas
you gave me for Christmas
hanging from the hook

on the bathroom door,
citron-scented bathwater,
and moth wings of steam

on the mirror.

This is enough:
To be alive and loved,
a little tipsy on white

zinfandel in a warm
tub without thinking
or wanting too much.

Similitude

After seeking the light's flame
and its mate in the mirror, a moth
the color of Chinese newspapers
perches on a small picture frame,

resting on that wooden ledge
for days. Finally, it dies, light
as a dried leaf above a print
of yellow butterflies.

Polishing Silver

I wish I could wipe clouds from the sky
like tarnish from a platter,

as the shaman makes rain
by scattering ashes in the wind.

If I draw a smiling face on the weeping
windowpane, will the sun come out again?

I rub the bruised tray
until I can see the moon

of my face in its clear surface,
wiping shadows from teaspoons,

fork tines, and the scrolled handles
of knives, controlling whatever

I can hold with sympathetic
magic, with internal weather.

Thumbnail Moon

On the drive home
tonight, pared to the least

light of morning's leavings,
the moon, the blue, even my breath

spread so thin that nothing's
left but this crone's

clipped nail, this bone
white emptiness.

Witch

She gazed in the mirror as a young girl
at her rosy, apple-cheeked twin,
staring until her face shifted into
a silver-haired woman's.

A trick of light refracted
from a sheet of mercury glass.
Still, it was a forecast—
the sharp, sunken cheeks

she would someday glimpse,
a woman staring back
in a shop window, a stranger
from another lifetime.

Mirror, mirror

From another lifetime
in a shop window, a stranger,
a woman staring back.
She would someday glimpse

the sharp, sunken cheeks.
Still, it was a forecast
from a sheet of mercury glass,
a trick of light refracted.

A silver-haired woman
staring until her face shifted into
the rosy, apple-cheeked twin
she saw in the mirror as a young girl.

What The Body Remembers

In your dream you write our children's names
on my back as I sleep beside you, my daughter's,
my son's, your daughter's, your grandson's,
and dates that are meaningful to us—
birthdays, the first day we made love.
I roll over (in the dream) and say,
You know I can't remember numbers!

But I remember your fingers
tracing cursive letters on my skin:
Martha. Noah. Sarah. Joe.
I pretend my hand is your hand
seeking the curvature within the O,
rewriting the end of our story
with a blue fountain pen.

And One More Thing ...

My mind races as I leave the house. What
if I forgot to lock the door? What if
I forgot to alphabetize the baby's blocks?
I should go back, just to be sure.

If I forgot to knock three times before locking the door,
I'll have bad luck. Did I wash my hands?
I should, just to be sure
I don't catch a flesh-eating strep infection.

I'll have bad luck if I don't wash my hands.
Better spray some Lysol on the phone, so
I don't catch bubonic plague or get a bad connection.
Did I forget to count the hairs in my brush?

Better say some lies on the phone, so
I can call in sick. I need to
since I forgot to count the stairs—I was in such a rush—
two, four, six, eight ...

I can call in sick. I need to
lick this teaspoon six times and tug on my ear or
clear my throat. *One, three, five, seven ...* Wait.
Did I recite the Lord's Prayer and

stick Post-it notes on the mirror?
I think I remembered, but maybe
I forgot to invite the German au pair
to dinner and didn't rewind *Monk.*

I think I remembered, but maybe
I didn't. Maybe I just thought I didn't.
Did I remind myself to toss out the junk
mail? I'll check once more in case

I didn't. Maybe I just thought I didn't.
My mind races as I lock the door. *What?*
I'll check once more just in case
I forgot to synchronize the clocks.

Beth Copeland lived in Japan, India, and North Carolina as a child. Her book *Traveling Through Glass* received the 1999 Bright Hill Press Poetry Book Award. Her poems have been widely published in literary journals and have received awards from *Atlanta Review, North American Review, The North Carolina Poetry Society,* and *Peregrine.* Two of her poems have been nominated for a Pushcart Prize. She is an English instructor at Methodist University in Fayetteville, North Carolina. She lives in a log cabin in the country with her husband, Phil Rech.

Made in the USA
Monee, IL
07 July 2026